The Taming of th...

AnD

A Selection of Illustrated Limericks

By

Zorba Tocks

Layout Design Collin Henry

Proofreader Georgina Mallalieu

Art Director and Editor Martin P. Crew-Gee

Order this book online at www.trafford.com or email orders@trafford.com

Most Trafford titles are also available at major book retailers.

Note for Librarians: A cataloguing record for this book is available from Library and Archives Canada at www.collectionscanada.ca/www.collectionscanada.ca/amicus/index-e.html

Printed in Victoria, BC, Canada.
ISBN 978-1-4251-8214-4 (soft)
ISBN 978-1-4251-8215-1 (e-book)

We at Trafford believe that it is the responsibility of us all, as both individuals and corporations, to make choices that are environmentally and socially sound. You, in turn, are supporting this responsible conduct each time you purchase a Trafford book, or make use of our publishing services. To find out how you are helping, please visit www.trafford.com/responsiblepublishing.htm

Our mission is to efficiently provide the world's finest, most comprehensive book publishing service, enabling every author to experience success. To find out how to publish your own book, your way, and have it available worldwide, visit us online at www.trafford.com

INTRODUCTION

The setting of the first story is an outrageous fantasy about domestic discipline between a Mother and her twin offspring who like to play and who are all consenting adults. You will need to imagine a lot more rest periods in - between the scenes than the story has allowed, because the punishments are given over a period of three hours. To heighten your fantasies, the players are nameless.

The second part of this book is a hilarious selection of fully illustrated short skits, describing each scene in verse form. The snappy rhythm of the verses focus on the pace of the stories and with cartoon illustrations, rhyme and rhythm are, to me, more effective than prose.

A short dictionary has been provided on some pages for the benefit of the audience outside English speaking countries and vice – versa. In particular, there are a lot of American words used that require explanation. Also, please read this book with an American accent, that is, with a short 'a' ("glass" not "gla(r)ss" as the British generally do), otherwise some words will not rhyme properly.

Pornographic and fetish images are neither in the book, nor will the use of child images or references to non – adult children appear in my books, in any form whatsoever.

This is the first of several theme books. Look out for more to come soon.

I hope you will all enjoy it and have a lot of fun.

Zorba Tocks

DEDICATION

This handmade 2 – in - 1 book is dedicated to all adults into the scene, or just curious, who like to read illustrated stories about chastisement, sometimes serious, but often funny.

My thanks go to all the people who encouraged me to write this book, for their good humor and continual support. Special thanks goes to Collin Henry for his professional services and to Georgina Mallalieu whose suggestions inspired me while creating this book. Without them it would not have reached publication. And thank you again Alicia, for cleverly inventing my pen name.

The Taming of the Twins

Written and illustrated
by
Zorba Tocks

THE REASONS

Some twins would spanking enact,
And were caught by their Mom in the act;
Now they'd been seen
They knew it would mean,
Punishment would soon be a fact.

Their Mother was not unkind,
But on this day they would find,
That whatever the age
Or development stage,
They would feel it on their behinds.

They had promised to do it no more,
Deserving punishment for sure
And as you will see,
The rewards will be,
Chastising events, oh so sore!

"Now, you are both twenty – one
And this should *not* be done!
But you fright me so,
I will make you glow
And this day by me will be won!"

"And other things I must stress!
Your rooms are a constant mess!
You promised you would
Clean – up as you should,
But *I* do the work and *you* less!"

"Then there is all your swearing,
That is needless and uncaring!
Those filthy words
Should *never* be heard,
And for that I'll be overbearing!"

Overbearing = aggressively masterful, in this case, to be severe.

THE ANTICIPATION

"I haven't spanked you for so long,
But I remember the discipline strong.
And I will enjoy
Many smacks to employ,
To obey rules and not do wrong!"

The beatings would leave them blue
And they did not know what to do.
To beg some conditions
For Moms renditions,
Or agree and pay the price due?

Said the brother, a naughty cad:
"It's okay from all that we've had.
We're her daughter and son
And spanking's such fun.
It really is not all that bad!"

His sister then blushed to a hue,
Said she: "Yeah, I like it too;
We know that because,
We don't have to pause
To choose what we already knew."

So they both decided to share,
Without so much as a care,
The harsh discipline
With a laugh and a grin
And Moms decision to bear.

"By the way, when the spankings are done,
You will find the results no fun!
For it's *me* in charge
And so by and large,
I will give you a painful *sum*!"

Two hours after supper was fed,
She ordered the twins to a bed.
"Now you'll both pray
For an end to this day!"
As them to the bedroom she led.

She pulled their clothing down
And eyed their rears with a frown,
"Both round and pink"
She said with a wink.
"I will teach you not to clown!"

"I've not seen your butts for a time,
And must say they both look divine.
But sorry you'll be,
When over my knee;
You won't find *anything* fine!"

9

THE PATHOS BEGINS

"There will be no need for thanks,
When I begin with hand spanks!"
And with her tough hands,
Their bottoms fanned
And also inflamed their flanks.

They were given each forty slaps
But they laughed somewhat from the taps.
While acting all coy
They writhed with such joy,
As the warm – up left no gaps.

Fanned – in this instance, spanking fast, like the quick movement of a fan

Flanks – sides of the buttocks

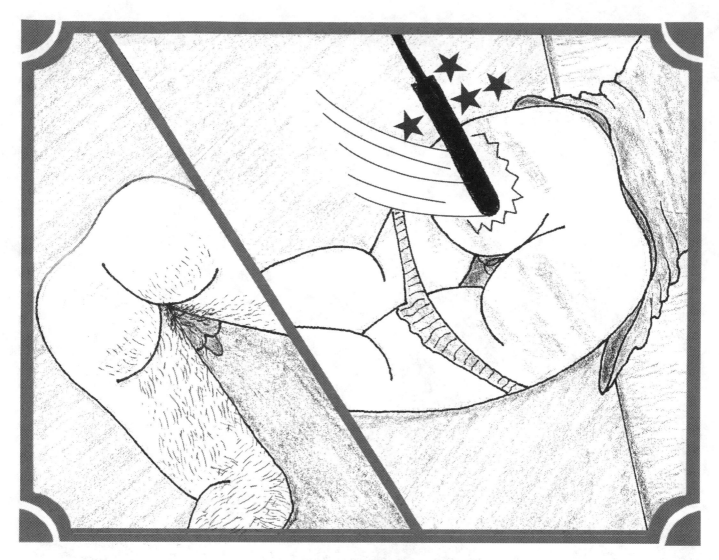

"My mind has already been set.
With each implement you'll get,
A good twenty – one
On each side of your bum,
And they'll **hurt a lot, you can bet!**"

"And now I will use these straps,
To lay into some hefty raps!
To stop your grins,
A light one that begins,
Then a heavy one for your lapse!

The light, narrow strap, landed square,
Starting softly which was fair.
There were oohs and sighs,
But there were no cries.
So far, it felt good down there.

*Landed square – the full width landed perfectly
aimed on their bottoms*

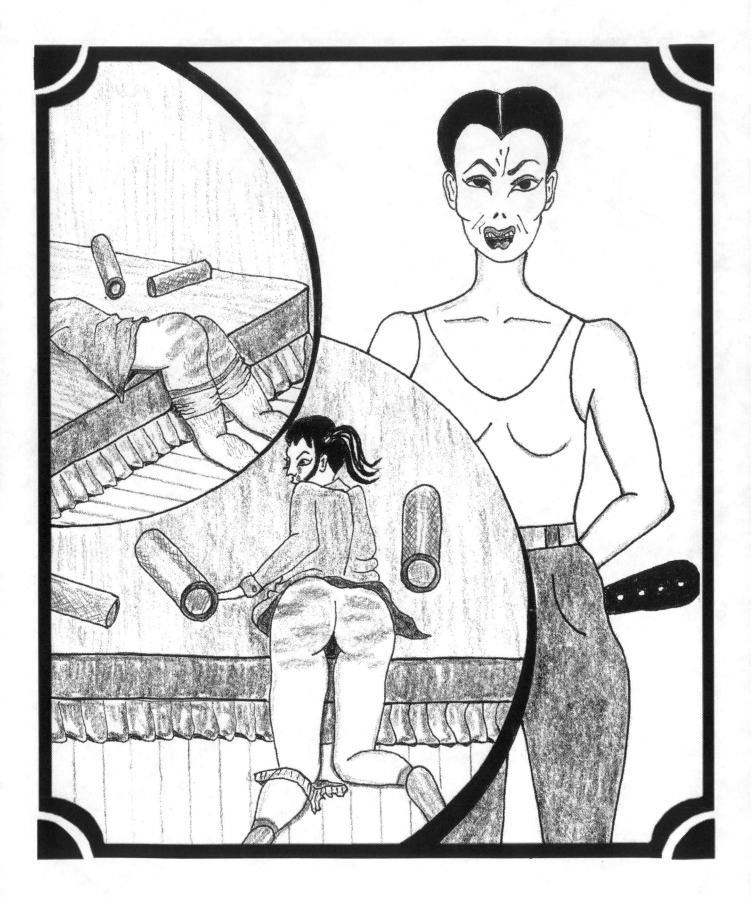

But the long one fell with such might,
That each one shuddered with fright;
She was a keen lasher
And soon became rasher
Making more mournful their plight.

She decided to rest for a bit,
As sparks on their bums had been lit.
Because even though earned,
Their bottoms which squirmed
Must remain a prime target to hit.

"I will have to continue to blame you,
To teach you sorrow and shame you!"
So she went to her rack
And with paddles came back
To make their bums black and blue.

"You will be extremely addled
After you have been paddled!"
And with some spite,
With their bums tight,
The whacks made their poor legs waddle.

The paddles were floppy and round,
That made a loud slapping sound
And covered their asses,
With severe passes
And their bottoms moved around.

Addled = confused

Waddle = like walking with short, swaying steps (their legs moving through the air)

15

Their buttocks became deeper red,
And in places dark blue instead,
It stung very much
And they wriggled and such,
Then stood and got off the bed.

"That was a mistake!" Mom said.
"I told you **both** to stay on the bed!
You will no more lay,
And now you will pay!
You will bend on your knees instead!"

They both knew they were in a mess,
When she said: "*Completely undress!*"
Since they were bold,
They did as she told,
But were humbled nevertheless.

"Now *obey* my words to the letter,
Otherwise you'll get *worse*, not better!
Hold each other down
So your bums are round,
Or else you'll be bound with a fetter!"

"*And now you will both really learn!*"
Mom shouted, with her voice stern.
"A cane on your butts
Will welt and leave ruts
And the strokes will certainly burn!"

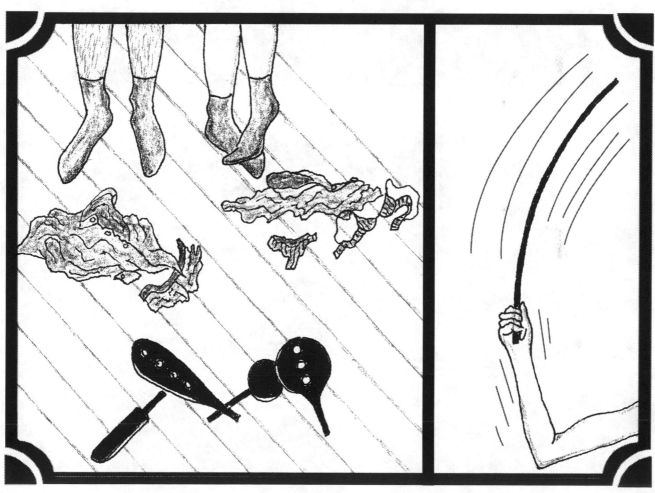

POOR, POOR TWINS!

The swishes and whops were just right,
As she caned them into the night,
Making them worry
Without any hurry,
Thrashing both hard and light.

Every blow fell with a crack,
No matter which side she'd whack.
With each purple weal,
They began to feel,
Their bottoms under fiery attack.

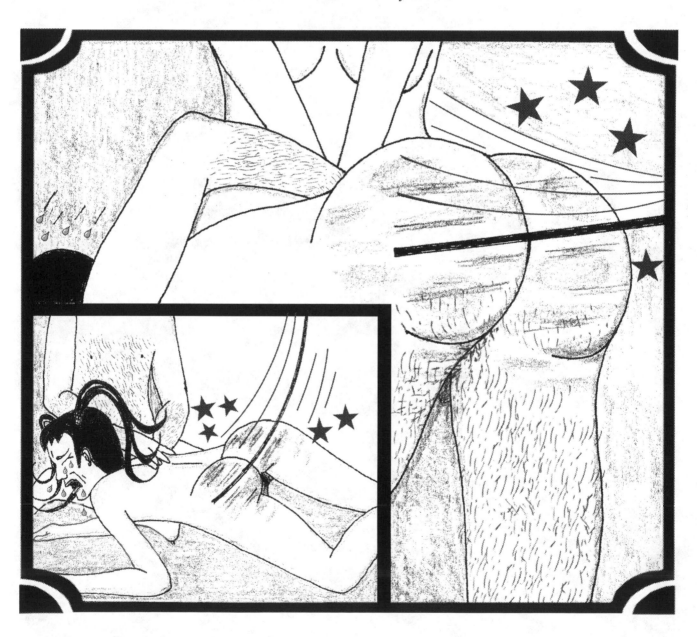

19

BUT THEN.....

"You misbehaved in my house
And this time I'll use a tawse!
I'll give you some more
Lying on the floor
And you'll tremble like a mouse!"

And lying prostrate with high bums,
With boosters under their tums,
With increasing fear,
It was made clear,
That the ending was not to come.

By now they were shaking in vain,
From the increasing and terrible pain.
And wished most strong,
They had not done wrong,
For the discipline when they had lain.

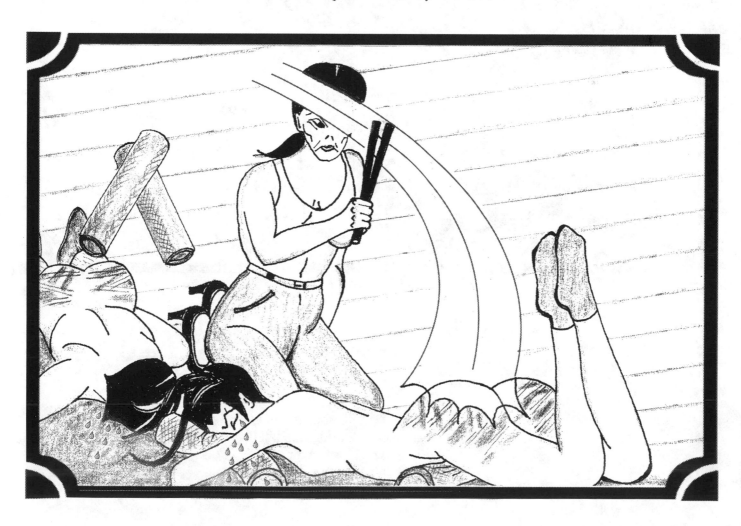

Tums — childlike word for tummy, stomach
Lying — same as laying (not meaning a falsehood)

While they were both lying bare,
Mom moved to her old wooden chair.
With them at a loss,
She would show who was boss
And spank them again right there.

"You are learning your lessons quite well
And by the time comes midnight's bell,
You'll know I'll not savor
Your bad behavior
And the ending will ***hurt like hell!***"

An O.T.K spanking as a grand finale is favored by some players to show complete domination and submission.

It was the brother who would be
The first to be over her knee,
She smacked his sore bot
Very hard and a lot,
Until she let him go free.

Mom is wearing Spanking Gloves (Mitts). The palms are lined with ¼ inch (6mm) of leather.
Bot = familiar abbreviation of "bottom".

AND POOR, POOR SIS...

But her daughter, watching the while,
Was seen hiding a silly smug smile.
And for her trouble
Got brutally double,
To teach her not to beguile.

They had both cried and screamed,
For that spanking it seemed,
Was worse than before
And they wanted no more,
For their buttocks were marred and sheened.

They were both full of dreadful rue,
With wet eyes swollen too;
And felt horribly rotten
For all they had gotten,
As their Moms threat had come true.

But despite their Moms severe rule,
They had never viewed her as a fool.
Although they had sobbed
When their bums had bobbed,
They cherished her like a fine jewel.

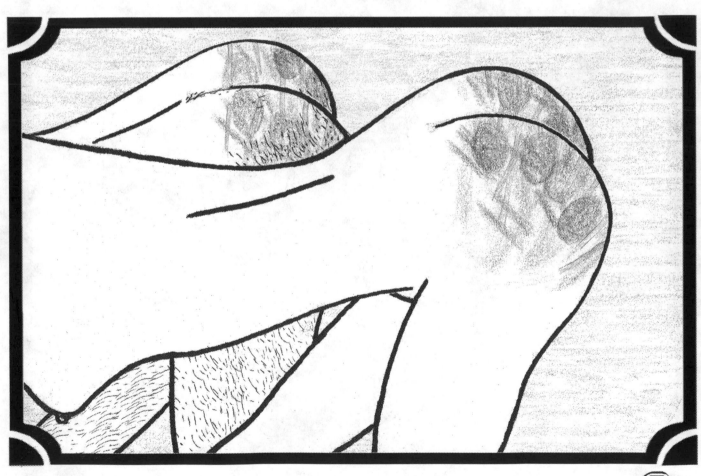

Sheened — "shining" as a result of the punishments
Bobbed — moved up and down
Cherished — to hold dear, loved

26

But she knew their passion defied,
All the efforts she had tried,
For they had gleaned
What she had dreamed
And would be to the family tied.

"Remember this," she said with a hiss,
"And put it on memories list.
You are never too old
To be spanked, I'm told!"
And then gave both hugs and a kiss.

"So that was the final ending
And a lesson I am defending.
But if *ever again*
You deserve more pain,
Its *over again* you'll be bending!"

THE END

Gleaned – gathered info and learnt from it

Coming soon:

THE
ADVENTURES
OF
SWANKY

SPANKTASTIC FUN!

A Selection of Illustrated Limericks

Spanking good skits

Written and illustrated
by
Zorba Tocks

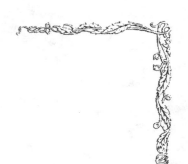
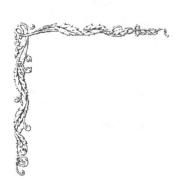

INDEX

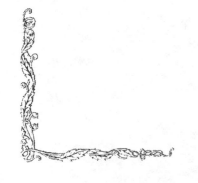
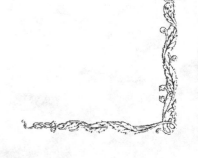

A Senior Senator

A senior Senator called Sandy,
Had a husband daft and dandy,
So she sat on his tummy
And batted his bummy
With a paddle she found very handy.

His unfortunate name was Orny
And Sandy was kinky and porny.
She gave him a strapping
To get his ass flapping,
Because it made him horny.

But her really most famous feat,
Was to cane him precise and neat,
Up and across
To his sorry loss,
As her games he could not defeat.

Tummy = stomach
Bummy = bottom, buttocks

The Messy Wife

A nice girl who thought like a flossie,
Loved her bubble baths all sloshy;
She liked sex in the tub
And would rub and scrub,
Until her front and behind were all glossy.

Her not caring was profound,
With a dreadful mess all around,
And she liked to play
Nearly every day,
And bent over was usually found.

But her man from the bathroom door,
Saw how wet was the entire floor.
So he took a back scrubber
And spanked her to blubber,
But she nevertheless cried for more.

Flossie = floozy, prostitute
Sloshy = in this sense, slushy with bubbles, splashing
Blubber = to cry noisily

A Lady Remiss

There once was a lady remiss,
For being disdainful and diss,
Tamed over a knee,
She no longer felt free,
To insult anymore with a hiss.

A "hiss" is a sibilant sound.
But when spanking comes around,
Sounds more like: "Shisst!"
Than: "Madame you misst!"
She didn't, when her pants were downed.

She was punished hard and a lot,
Until deep red was her bot.
As each whack was felled,
She screamed and she yelled,
And remembered all that she'd got.

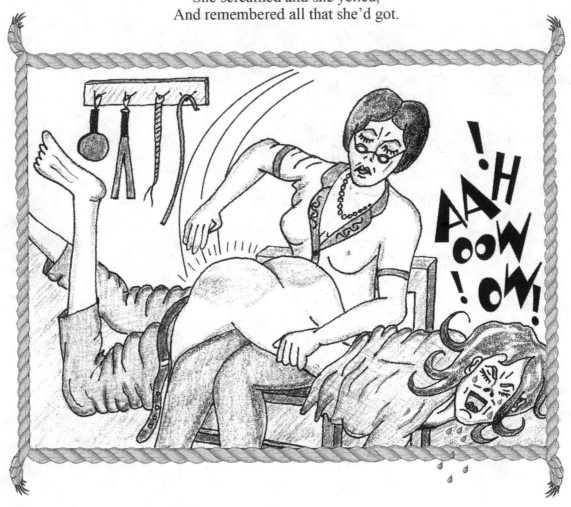

Sibilant = speaking through a small, narrow mouth.
Diss = to insult
Downed = fell (taken) down
Felled = hand spank coming down
Shisst = not a real word, sort of taken from scheisse = shit
Misst = not a real word, meaning missed

34

Bird the Nerd

There once was a nerd named Bird,
Who got e – mail from a girl he'd lured.
"You'll get a floggin'
When you log – in!"
She'd give him all he deserved.

So they fixed it to meet on a date,
And, of course, Bird the Nerd was late.
By the time that he came
She'd thought up a game,
For his timing had made her irate.

She multitasked very well
And, as far as she could tell,
Her new implements
Would download repents
And hurt Bird the Nerd like hell.

It all went as she planned with no bug
And lessons were learnt by that lug,
And when completed
With him defeated,
Gave his dick a programmed tug.

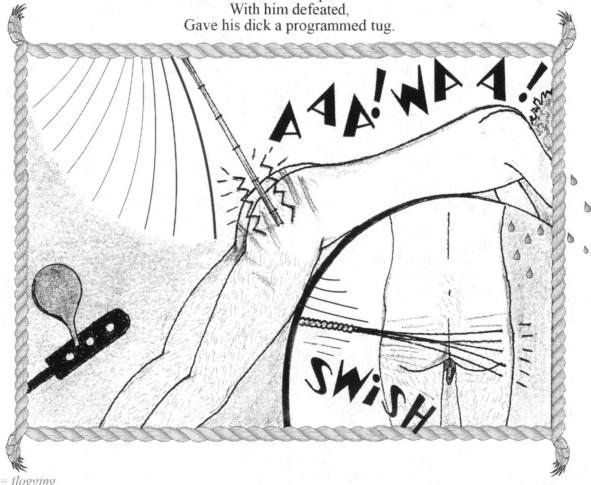

Floggin' = flogging
Inept = not suitable
Lug = idiot;
Tug = pull

A Simple Pimple

A gent from Ghent who was simple,
Thought he had a bad pimple.
He'd squeezed and pushed
And squashed it to mush,
But it turned out to be only a dimple.

His dominant wife, who was rich,
Could sometimes be a real bitch,
And tend to his ass
For having no class,
With a wicked whip and a switch.

She'd liked to sit upon him,
And whack him at her whim,
As naked she wielded
The lash 'til he yielded
And the white of his ass became dim.

So the lesson about a dimple,
Is not to see it as a pimple;
If squeezed and pushed
And squashed to a mush,
A good walloping will be simple.

Ghent = a city in Belgium.
Mush = like pulp, messy.
Dim = the white faded, not seen anymore

The Cozy Couple

There once was a girl from the Rhine,
Who found discipline very fine.
Hand spankings, then brushes,
Then straps gave her blushes,
And canings made her feel benign.

So she married a French guy from Brie
And she made him feel bold and free.
"It's just little me
Over your knee,"
Said she: "It's just how I be!"

"Ha, ha, hee, hee!" said the man from Brie,
"I can be in your place, you see!"
So upturned he went
'Til her spanks were spent
And they switched very happily.

That couple from Brie and the Rhine,
Decided that lust was divine;
Their hunger unsated
It was soon abated,
By dining on cheese and fine wine.

Benign = kind, meaning well – disposed, not aggressive (feeling)
Cozy = smug
Switched = changed places from a spanker to a spankee

The Switchers

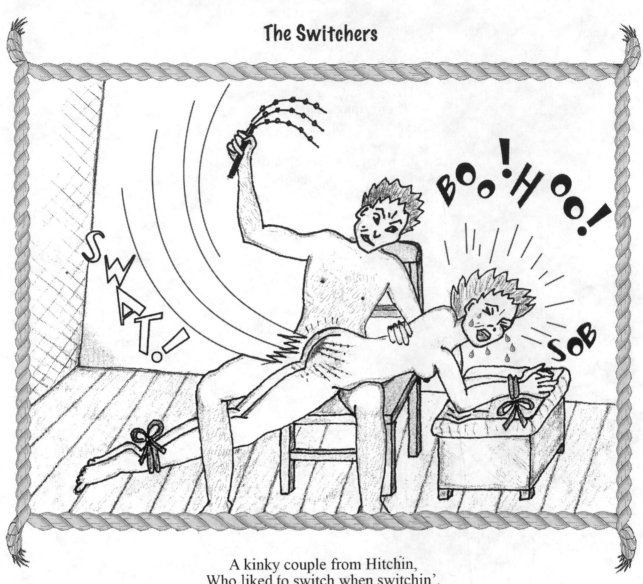

A kinky couple from Hitchin,
Who liked to switch when switchin',
Seemed always to know
From a mute secret glow
When desire for a switchin' was itchin'.

But the man was often a cad,
Very horrid and usually bad;
So, bent on a chair
Pants off and bare,
She laid – on the best he had had.

And when the young wife was a shrew,
The hard man knew well what to do;
He would tie her around
Then whip her sound
And when over, admire the view.

Shrew = bossy, bad tempered woman
Sound = thorough, as in 'a sound thrashing.'

A poet had problems with ictus,
That turned into a terrible sicktus.
She practiced the beat,
Upon her bare seat,
But nothing came out of her rictus.

"I have one solution," she thought
And went out to a shop and bought,
A length of rattan,
As she was a fan,
But sadly enough, self – taught.

She stripped all her clothes off at home
And aimed the long cane at her dome,
Then lashed each side
And the pain did abide,
'Til her rictus yelled the right tone.

Sicktus = not a word, means sickness; Self — Dom = a flagellant, self - discipline
Rictus = an expanse of an open mouth; Ictus = a poetical stress or beat.
Ictus and rictus together meaning she was trying to find a word with the right beat.
Abide = put up with

Hedwig the Bitch

A German who had a gay itch,
Was seeking a guy who was rich,
He had his sex changed,
Was married and named:
'Hedwig the Bitch' who got hitched.

One day she was in a bad flap
And he used a cane and a strap.
She deserved to be beat
Upon her rare seat,
Bent over her strong man's lap.

But she would quickly discover,
On her butt without any cover,
That when it stuck out
To get a good clout,
She enjoyed being spanked by her lover.

Bad flap = moody
Seat = bottom
Clout = smack

A Simple Pimple

A gent from Ghent who was simple,
Thought he had a bad pimple.
He'd squeezed and pushed
And squashed it to mush,
But it turned out to be only a dimple.

His dominant wife, who was rich,
Could sometimes be a real bitch,
And tend to his ass
For having no class,
With a wicked whip and a switch.

She'd liked to sit upon him,
And whack him at her whim,
As naked she wielded
The lash 'til he yielded
And the white of his ass became dim.

So the lesson about a dimple,
Is not to see it as a pimple;
If squeezed and pushed
And squashed to a mush,
A good walloping will be simple.

Ghent = a city in Belgium.
Mush = like pulp, messy.
Dim = the white faded, not seen anymore

36

Bird the Nerd

There once was a nerd named Bird,
Who got e – mail from a girl he'd lured.
"You'll get a floggin'
When you log – in!"
She'd give him all he deserved.

So they fixed it to meet on a date,
And, of course, Bird the Nerd was late.
By the time that he came
She'd thought up a game,
For his timing had made her irate.

She multitasked very well
And, as far as she could tell,
Her new implements
Would download repents
And hurt Bird the Nerd like hell.

It all went as she planned with no bug
And lessons were learnt by that lug,
And when completed
With him defeated,
Gave his dick a programmed tug.

Floggin' = flogging
Inept = not suitable
Lug = idiot;
Tug = pull

The Old Man's Chagrin

There once was a wife who was pushy,
Who spanked her old man's bare tushy.
When she did it with ardor,
She spanked him much harder,
Until his poor tushy went mushy.

For more fun and part of foreplay,
She whacked on and off for a day
And quite as expected,
He became erected,
Cried: "Eureka!" and knelt down to pray.

"Don't waste any time down there,"
She said, while undressing with care.
Then to his chagrin,
His penis went in
And got lost in his pubic hair.

Ardor = intensity of emotion, enthusiasm
Tushy = bottom, buttocks
Eureka = used to express triumph or discovery
Chagrin = to humiliate

An S & M – ish Couple

A young couple, who were Flemish,
Thought themselves quite S & M – ish,
Until a time came,
To name not a name,
When one butt was a gory blemish.

So they opted for soft B & D
And would bind one another with glee;
But who was which
To get the switch,
Was a toss of a Euro, you see.

But the vrouw had a clever head
And thought up a plan instead,
A coin with two heads
So her man would be led,
Always, with him tied to the bed.

Bum Dust

There once was a man named Ott,
Who spanked with a large fly – swat.
It caused a fracas,
When it flew off an ass
And made him feel like a clot.

Using anything else made him queasy,
But he did not give up so easy,
And found much neater
A long carpet beater,
That became for his gal a good teasey.

But he got a surprise one day,
When to his greatest dismay,
His gal got fussed
When out flew dust
From her bum he beat ev'ry – which – way.

Fracas = ado
Teasey = warm – up
Fussed = very concerned
Ev'ry = shortening of every
Every – which – way = all over

Edwina's Scena'

There once was a gal named Edwina,
Who yearned for a sexy spank scena',
With her bottom bared
While her partner dared,
To cane her with a dildo betweena'.

For she had a hot fire insida'
And could in her man confida',
To be spanked in a rush
With a wooden brush,
Until hot enough he could rida'.

A Happy Fate

A gent whose secret nourishment,
Required regular corporal punishment,
Had a wife who discovered
A strap in his cupboard,
To be used without much encouragement.

He taught very well how to cure
And how much he could endure.
Having finished with that,
They had not a spat;
She made him feel utterly pure.

When a few weeks had gone by
She'd heard from her man not a cry.
So increased her whams
Using both hands
And his pleasure was hard to deny.

After all that said and done,
With practice a lot on his bum,
She felt really great
For his happy fate
And gave merrily more a good sum.

Cure = made to feel better.
Spat = small argument.
Funs = playful enjoyments.
Buns = buttocks.
A good sum = a lot of smacks, a great amount of discipline
Whams = to hit with a loud noise

45

Sweet Spanks

A sweet – toothed lady did tricks,
With a whip made of licorice sticks.
Then lashing a bum
Made it sticky and numb,
That she slurped with slobbery licks.

But her cutey who was named Mandy,
And who often was naughty and randy,
Had a bottom so sweet,
That she liked to beat,
With a long, hard yard of candy.

Licorice = a sweet, black, herbal soft candy
Slurped = to eat or drink noisily
Slobbery = letting saliva drool from the mouth

The Tawsing

There once was a guy named Rownd,
Who was for London bound.
He wanted to spank,
A visiting Yank,
But there wasn't one to be found.

He then met a Brit called Sable,
Who had a sister named Mabel,
Then in a motel,
He tawsed them well,
Bending over a wooden table.

'Though Sable cried louder than Mabel,
And Mabel cried longer than Sable,
They both said when done
With their buttocks numb:
"We'll all meet again when able."

Bound = going towards
Tawse = a traditional Scottish implement made of usually two wide, thick and long lashes of leather.

A Lady Bored

A lady as hard as a board,
Braided a lash of whip-cord,
She thrashed herself quick
Because her man Vic,
Was away and she was bored.

When finally home he did come,
His knee he put under her tum.
'Though she was a self – dom,
She got hot and on,
When he paddled her blistering bum

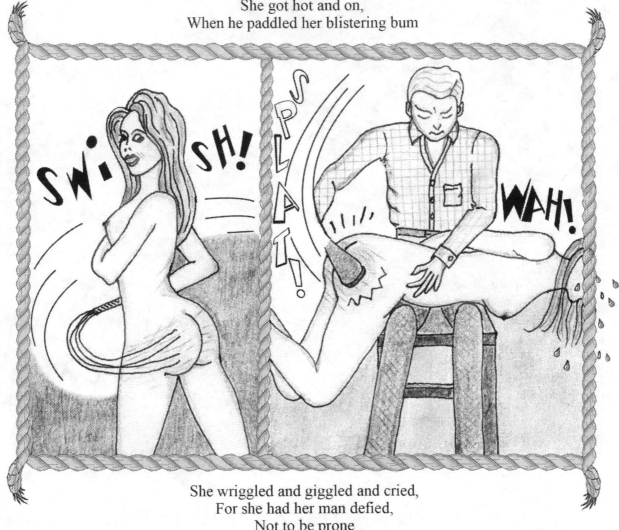

She wriggled and giggled and cried,
For she had her man defied,
Not to be prone
To do it alone,
Nor hide it when she had lied.

Lying to him was her pleasure,
For a spanking at his leisure,
She was a bad lass
But found it a gas
To have a sore butt to treasure.

48

Miss Vext

There once was a vixen named Vext,
Who wrote naughty and sexual text.
But every word,
Sounded absurd,
So was spanked for being too sext.

I will tell you what happened next,
With a whipping rod curved and flexed.
The curve of the rod,
Was the same as her bod
And the spanker became perplexed.

The spanker, a dame with wrong glasses,
Thought that Miss Vext had two asses,
And try as she might,
Such was her sight,
That the dame could only swish passes.

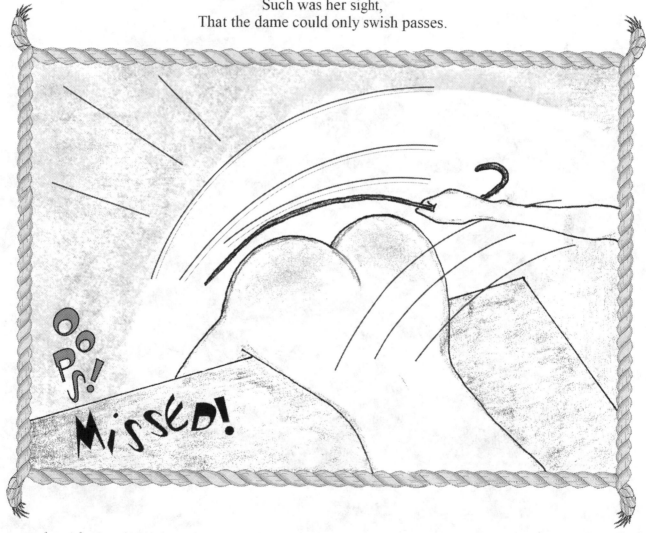

Vixen = a shrewish, swearing woman
Miss Vext = meaning Miss Angry
Sext = not a word, but intends to mean 'too sexy.'
Bod = slang for body

A Lady Dubbed Dawn

There once was a soft luscious botty,
That was spanked very hard and a lotty.
Until one day,
In the month of May,
It was black and blue and looked grotty.

It belonged to a lady dubbed Dawn,
Who was always feeling forlorn
And wanted the slipper
From a very good whipper,
Laid bare outside on a lawn.

She met a nice guy named Jon,
Who came from the city of Bonn.
He gave her what for,
But she asked for more;
That's the reason they get on.

Botty = childish word for bottom
Lotty = a nonsense word meaning 'a lot.'
Grotty = wretched, messy and not nice.
Dubbed = named, called Dawn

Silly Willy

An American wife named Filly,
Was forced to do something silly,
Her man had got caught
In a mousetrap he bought
And she had to cut off his willy.

Down to the Doc's he did rush,
Was stitched and looked like a bush,
Down there he had nought
And the trouble it brought
Made him lose all his thrust and push.

His wife was really surprised
When the impact he realized
And asked for a spank
From his lovely Yank
And then to be feminized.

Now, the wife had certainly tried,
But whenever he pouted and cried,
A spanking she would
Give him real good,
For the silly willy that died.

Willy = penis
Nought = also naught, meaning 'nothing'.

51

Yikkity - Yack

There once was a lady named Yenta,
Who was known as a very rich renter.
But she gossiped so much
And during sex would not touch,
So her husband paid twice not to enter.

But one day her yikkity – yack,
Behind her husbands back,
Got her heinie
Whacked with a wienie
And then she was given the sack.

Yenta = gossipy woman
Yikkity — Yack = nonsense words meaning chatter, talking too much
Heinei = buttocks, bottom
Weinie = a sausage
Given the sack = here it means got her out of the house, divorced

Big Beautiful Bum

There once was a lady who hobbled
As she walked and twaddled and bobbled.
She had an ass like a duck,
That would clean all the muck,
When her buttocks bounced and wobbled.

Her idol had spanked her nates,
From their very first few dates;
They were large and round
And would him astound,
When they went in and out at fast rates.

She wanted her butt to lose weight,
But he thought it was too late.
"They are good as they are
And better by far
Than buttocks that carry no freight."

Hobbled = to limp, walk in an awkward way
Bobbled = to fumble, clumsy
Twaddle = talked foolishly
Wobbled = to move unsteadily
Freight = in this sense a large amount (of bottom)

Twosome and Threesome

There once was a lady named Jade,
Who loved to be spanked with a spade.
But after forty
Got happily naughty,
Then liked to be thoroughly laid.

She was just like her friend Nancy,
Whose husband's name was Clancy,
Who found it a breeze
When over his knees,
Because it tickled her fancy.

But when they had a threesome,
(Which is fun when you can see some),
They switched and clowned
And jumped all around
With results that were often gleesome.

The Nymph

There once was a wife twee and twiggy,
Whose buttocks were wantonly wriggly.
Her mans hand took care,
Of everything there
And that made her jerky and jiggley.

Her appetite liked nothing finer
Than to use a dildo in a diner,
But once with a poke
The damn thing broke
And the tag read: "Made from China'.

So for being a nymph and prissy
And a spoilt and impish missy,
Her botty was bashed,
For sex that was rash,
And for being insatiably kissy.

Twiggy = small
Wriggly & jiggley = sexy movements of her derriere, however, they should not be spelt with a 'y' ending.
Wantonly = behaving badly
Prissy = very proper, too polite, in a sense snobbish
Insatiable = not being able to be satisfied, continually wanting more.

A Stupid Mutt

There once was a masochist sinner,
Who asked his Dom lady to dinner.
When it was done,
She flogged his bum
And both turned out as a winner.

But then he started to moan
While refusing to really atone,
Put over her knees,
He was smacked 'til he sneezed
And to never again misatone.

But the idiot would not keep shut,
So she taught him upon his butt,
36 with a cane
For being profane
And for being a stupid mutt.

Keep shut = keep quiet, close his mouth
Mutt = a mongrel dog (mixed breed) but means 'idiot' or 'dope' when applied to humans

Kushi's Sushi

A Japanese lady named Kushi,
Who of course, ate lots of sushi,
Was showy and dishy
When hit with a fishy,
As it gave her a colorful tushy.

Her husband whose name was Korum,
Loved to spank her with decorum.
But she liked it more,
Kneeling on the floor,
And playing the scene in a forum.

He forcefully beat without care,
His Carp on her neat derriere.
That fat bony fish,
Came down with a swish,
And bashed her scaly bum bare.

Tushy = buttocks, bottom
Swish = the sound of an implement (cane, strap, etc) as it comes down through the air
Fwishy = not a word, a play on fish and swish
Scaly = the shiny scales of the fishes skin stuck to her bum.
Carp = a long lived fresh water fish
Bashed = hit hard

Tutors x 3

A teacher named Picky Pickering,
Was often ranting and bickering.
'Til a female professor,
Vied to undress her
And gave her butt a good lickering.

One of the others, named Dikkers,
Teased with bad sways and flickers.
So they made her blubber,
With a whip made of rubber,
After pulling down her red knickers.

Bickering = arguing
Lickering = not a word, a play on the word 'licking', a beating
Blubber = to cry noisily

The Birching

There once was a Swede from Boras,
Who her man thought was a strong lass.
When he said the wrong thing,
It was so sure to bring,
Many screams when she lashed his ass.

She favored a freshly cut birch
Right after service at church,
And with her long arm
She flogged with no charm
And made his poor body lurch.

Her boyfriend asked her to be kind,
And not to whip his behind.
When she did it a lot,
He got sexily hot
And now finds himself in a bind.

Hot = in this sense from the punishment that made him feel randy
In a bind = meaning a problem, because he did not want it before, but now he thinks he likes it.

A Golden Touch

There once was a lady named Phollys,
Who was stropped for her silly follies,
By a very old guy,
Who was otherwise shy,
For he wanted to get up his jollies.

She liked the old geezer and such,
As he thrashed with a golden touch,
He would hit soft and long
And nothing went wrong
And she loved all the taps very much.

He held her in place with a fetter,
But she always found it much better,
If spanked she could be,
Spread over his knee,
Until she was red and much wetter.

Follies = folly, silliness
Get up his jollies = in this sense, get sexually excited and erect
Geezer = an eccentric (odd) man, usually old
Fetter = a shackle, example hand cuffs

60

Gerda and Hilda

But before we go any furda,
You should hear all about Gerda.
Spanked at midnight,
She yelled with delight
And all the neighbors hearda.

A Dom, who was named Tuppa,
Had slapped her hard after supper,
And her bottom felt nice
Beat 30 times thrice
And gave her a really good uppa.

But when flogged by her friend Hilda,
Who was very strongly willda,
She was made to bend
And off her clothes rend,
For a beating that nearly killda.

61

Bent from Incest

A man who thought he knew best,
Was incurably bent from incest.
He had married his Sis,
But the ass he would kiss,
Was his gay Bro disguised as a jest.

But the Sis did not like the jokes
And decided to whip both the blokes.
Since one was Bi
And the other a lie,
Their patooties would feel the strokes.

So all of their clothing was shed
And they waited on a bed.
And to their bane,
She wielded a cane.......
And all of them knew where it led.

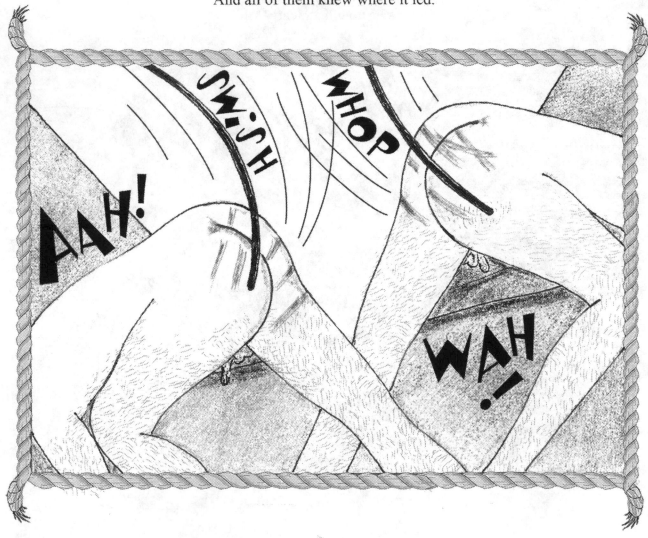

Incest = sexual intercourse with a related person
Pattooties = buttocks
Bane = a cause of misery, worry

Dill Pickle

An egoist who was blatant and fickle,
Used his penis for slap and tickle.
But he became vexed,
When he married a Hex
And she made it become a Dill Pickle.

And to make worse his sorry face,
She took him to a secret place,
For some potion sipping
And dungeon whipping,
To enforce his dopey disgrace.

She beat him exacting and slow,
Until he squawked like a crow,
But was suddenly lewd
And extremely crude,
When she gobbled his poor dildo.

Blatant = obvious
Fickle = not loyal
Slap and tickle = foreplay
Vexed = angry
Hex = a witch, also a magic spell
Dill Pickle = preserved gherkin, a zucchini variety;
Gobbled = ate quickly

Coming soon:

THE
ADVENTURES
OF
SWANKY

In "The House of Discipline," an old Victorian mansion owned by the Family Grob, Swanky, the daughter, is taught first to be submissive and then graduates to become a Dominatrix. She experiences, as others do as well, pain and laughter and sadness and happiness during her many severe trials and tribulations.

It is a romantic story about domestic and traditional discipline. Written in prose and enhanced by endearing illustrations, an aura of intimate allure is cast that will encourage the reader to empathize with, and love, the characters.

The following pages have been extracted as a taster………..

……………………….. It was early evening when Swanky walked into the lounge, looking as pretty as a spring day and cheerfully pleased to greet her parents. At twenty – eight years of age, she had matured into a superbly attractive woman with an allure about her that was irresistible.

"Hi Mama and Papa," she said in her Anglo accent with a hint of French pronunciation that had a unique and pleasant Quebec ring to it: "What's up?"

"How was your day at the Law Office?" Virgina asked her.

"Ugh!" pouted Swanky: "Mama, I find it increasingly difficult to defend guilty people. They seem to show no remorse. I know it is naïve to think this, but I simply believe that if you are guilty you should admit it and pay the price. Now I have to work all night preparing arguments to prove my guilty client is as pure as the driven snow!"

Virgina exchanged a furtive glance at Fallus and a small smile lit her face. "Swanky," she said in a persuasive tone of voice: "sit down my Dear; we have a proposition to make to you."

She sat on one of the sofas and waited while her father brought her a Martini. The lounge was one of their favorite rooms to sit in and chat. It still had the original Victorian windows and wood paneling and surrounds that had been carefully preserved. It was chilly outside and they felt snug tucked away in their enormous old house in the area of Mount Royal, in Montreal.

Virgina, a truly beautiful woman, took a sip of her drink and coughed slightly to clear her throat before she began to explain their proposition………………………..

................Grandmother Molly MacMasterly possessed an austere visage that belied her generosity of spirit. With her black hair gray now, there was still a wicked twinkle in her eyes that both Virgina and Swanky had inherited. "Be patient," Molly advised: "learn your lessons well and the quicker the better for your own sake. The sooner you complete the course, the sooner you will be taught the arts of discipline. When you are satisfactory, your mother and Dilly Doe will introduce you to your first clients."

"You always make things sound so easy Nana," Swanky said, which made Molly strut a bit as she went to refresh the coffee urn.

Molly repeated some of the family history that Swanky knew by heart, but was polite enough to pretend to listen avidly. Molly's cousin from Edinburgh had immigrated to London, England, after having severe difficulties finding a secure and well paid job that suited her qualifications as a sales person. When she got there, she encountered similar obstructions and drastically decided to change her career. Eventually, she supported a house in Hampstead from her profitable earnings as a Dominatrix. It was she who had persuaded Molly to do the same thing.

Molly was a canny, practical and determined Scot who had always been a strict disciplinarian, as her upbringing had been tough when she learnt from an early age to respect the harshness of the tawse. She had often spanked Virgina and Prissy, her daughters, for their errors, but only once gave them both a quick punishment with the tawse, as they behaved well and seldom deserved it, except on that one occasion when they had been overly objectionable. It was not too difficult for her to make the transition to become a Dominatrix, as she had concluded that the rewards far outweighed alternative possibilities. Consequently, she had sent her children to stay with relatives while her cousin had visited for a few weeks to train her, an experience that she had found acceptable but exceptionally painful on the fresh tenderness of her rump; but, nevertheless necessary if she was to learn properly and make a success of herself.

After Swanky and Hans Summ, her brother, were born, she decided to retire as a Dominatrix and handed the business and house over to Virgina, whom she had severely trained herself before they had come along. She was very happy running about the place, commanding the kitchen and looking after her grand - children.

So there it was, two generations of professionals in the same family, ready to pass the business on to a third generation, although Swanky was not aware of it at the time.

Swanky stirred in her chair and wriggled her bottom on the seat. She was still not fully sure, but Molly had made her mentally comfortable, at least, by explaining the normality of it all. She was always amazed at her openness about her upbringing, spanking history and her feelings about them, especially how she regarded the House to be a positive and rewarding place to be................

.............................."Ouch! This is cruel!" cried Swanky: "How many more?"

"Twenty - eight, because you disobeyed and tried to stand!" insisted Dilly Doe: "And, we will build you up to take at least forty without moving or complaining!"

Swanky's eyes widened in horror at the thought of it as the punishment continued. Her entire bottom was red and blue and burned with a stinging throb. She could not help complaining and wanted Dilly Doe to stop. Instead, she compressed her lips as she clamped her teeth together. Virgina noticed and reminded her to breathe deeply and try to relax, as tensing the body only made it worse. That is OK for you to say, thought Swanky, now not daring to speak out loud.

Dilly Doe waited between each stroke to let them sink into her skin with meaningful instruction, until the last ones, that she termed "the sweetest of all." She waited for ten seconds, then raised her arm well above her shoulder and twice directed the implement with resounding effect upon each side of poor Swanky's pitiful behind, while she yelled from the pain as tears spurted from her eyes. That last performance was repeated three times before she was allowed to stand up. She screamed from the results and hopped from one leg to the other and continued to weep profusely while kneading her bottom with both hands to ease the pain.

Five minutes later, Virgina passed her clothes to her and stated in a matter – of – fact tone of voice: "Try to prepare yourself mentally tonight, because tomorrow you are going to be given a severe caning."

A tremor went through her body as she thought in awe of worsening punishment as she walked stiffly to her apartment. "I have apparently learnt something, but I will have to wait until later to figure that out!" she mumbled when she reached her bedroom.............................

Zorba Tocks

68